Go Through and Overcome

The Grief, Pain, and Pressure to Reclaim Your Purpose

Go Through and Overcome

The Grief, Pain, and Pressure to Reclaim Your Purpose

By

Rita A. Wallace Posey

XULON ELITE

Xulon Press Elite
2301 Lucien Way #415
Maitland, FL 32751
407.339.4217
www.xulonpress.com

Dedication

*I have been young, and now I'm a graybeard – not
once have I seen an abandoned believer, or his kids
out roaming the streets. Every day he's out giving and
lending, his children making him proud. Am old; yet I
have not seen the righteous forsaken;
Nor his descendants begging bread.*

(Psalm 37:25-26)

To my lovely children and grandchildren, who suffered with me through our loss, I am so proud of your faith and trust in God. You have all courageously continued on with your lives.

To my husband's friends and colleagues, when what was received as true, you wanted to believe anything other than what was being said. Convinced that things happened too suddenly, left with many unanswered questions, or never had the opportunity to say your personal goodbyes. Be not uneasy, for your unspoken words were felt in his heart, he knew, and he cared so much about everyone. His greatest concern was not to worry anyone. He was remarkably brave and strong, he kept the faith, ran his race, and fought a good fight. He would always sing a few lyrics from an old gospel song, "It Ain't Over Until God Says It's Over." To you all, please be at peace.

Let me broaden this dedication to include all who have suffered the loss of a loved one. My prayer is that you hold on to your memories and boldly continue to live a limitless life far beyond your wildest dreams.

> *There's an opportune time to do things, a right time*
> *for everything on the earth; A right time for birth and*
> *another for death, To everything there is a season, a time*
> *for every purpose under the heaven; A time to be born,*
> *and a time to die.*

(Ecclesiastes 3:1-2)

When all is said and done, you are part of me. That's the way it
was meant to be.
People are brought together for a reason, everything happens
for a reason.
I believe the reason you and I were brought together was
because we complete one another.
We fill in each other's missing spots with love.
And if someday God decides to tear us apart, I trust that there
is a reason.
'Cause if there is a reason for love, there is a reason for life
beyond it.

—Unknown

Acknowledgments

To my loving son and daughter, Lydell and Lanita, thank you both for your love that has no end. You both gave me a rib when mine could not be mended. You held my hand through the storm and rocked me to sleep because things were no longer the norm. You both handled things with such bravery, and you showered me with constant love without end. I am truly blessed to also call you both my friends!

To my dearest sisters, Renita and Priscilla, and my special friend, Yvonne Montgomery, thank you all for ministering to my brokenness. You welcomed me into your home (at any hour) when I didn't want to go to my own. You cooked and served me meals when I couldn't for myself. You stood in the gap and prayed when I couldn't pray for myself. You protected my shattered pieces and kept the faith, because you knew that soon and very soon, I would be restored, renewed, and rebirthed to reclaim my purpose. Your wonderful hearts helped me to keep it together, to walk through the valley and not sit.

To my dearest niece, LaTasha, during a pivotal time in your own life, a time when you needed all your strength and reserve for yourself, you managed to stand as a pillar of strength for me. For you had suffered the loss of your beloved mom, my sister a few months prior to me losing my beloved husband. Yet, when the Lord asked, "Whom shall I send?" You answered, "Send me, I'll go!" Your wise, sweet spirit is unexplainable. It's almost as if you've walked these grounds before. You taught me how to laugh again and pushed me out of my four walls of darkness. Thank you for taking all my calls and showing up at my front door at every perfect moment!

To my precious cousin, Janette, thank you for the pen you used to craft several years of handwritten messages, and for your ministering tongue. You guarded my emptiness and guided my way. I embraced your healing message every Friday. I am forever grateful!

To my strong niece, Valerie, thank you for being the voice when I didn't have a voice. You covered my back while I wasn't aware of all the attacks. You were even willing to be ostracized by many just for me. Thank you for your strength, kindness, encouragement, and support over the years. You kept me grounded and enabled me to finish this book!

Endorsements

"Go Through and Overcome–The Grief, Pain, and Pressure to Reclaim Your Purpose" offers a vision of healing and encouragement as you may discover your purpose in life through your storms, trials, and tribulations. Rita has eloquently shared her story how with God she has been able to journey through her desert and overcome the grief, pain, and pressure to reclaim her purpose. For when you trust in God, joy cometh in the morning.

-Maxine Griffin Somerville, Chair, Charles County
Commission for Women

Before I begin my review, I want to say thank you to the author for sharing her path to discovery. In life, we always try to avoid the talks about death which forces us to figure it out, oftentimes alone, when a loved one is taken away. The personal journey shared in "Go Through and Overcome – The Grief, Pain, and Pressure to Reclaim Your Purpose" helped me to see what I went through as a natural process we all will one day experience. This book will help you find that silver lining in what seems like a dark reality with no purpose in sight. It is so touching that the journey through this book takes you beyond the mourning and grief right to your purpose. As a Christian and a believer, I know that God never gives us more than we can bear. The caring, personal, and sentimental encouragement within the pages of this book is confirmation that death of a loved one is not meant to break us, but rather guide us through a process where we, too, will discover a purpose for that pain. Beautiful Read!

-LaTasha Briscoe, Owner and Creative Director

Table of Contents

Preface

By God's grace, I pray every reader finds peace and comfort from the words written in this self-help memoir. It is designed to help you *Go Through* a difficult season. While no one is immune from life storms, brokenness, or unforeseen battles; no one should ever have to go through them alone. I am hopeful this memoir supplies a means of support, and will inspire and encourage those who have found themselves struggling to move on after the death of a loved one. May the message, pictures, and prayers found in this self-help memoir minister to your needs and challenges as I share my love story.

My need to be at the water was where I gathered my sudden strength to write. It was where I found my meet-up with the Lord. Throughout my journey, each scenery shown, provided a breathless backdrop as I shared my struggles, and finally, my survival.

"There's an opportune time to do things, a right time for everything on the earth: A right time for birth and another for death. To everything there is a season, a time to be born, And a time to die..." (Ecclesiastes 3:1-2 NKJV). Your life assignment does not end when a loved one perishes, nor should you bury yourself in the valley of despair. Even in the midst of heartbreak, one must cling to life to either discover, reclaim or revive his or her godly purpose. I am with you. Our Father created, mandated, and established our life purpose. He deposited the dream, the plan, and the purpose for our destiny—the dates for life and death. I thank God that He favored my days to go through and overcome the grief, pain, and pressure to reclaim my purpose.

INTRODUCTION

What Is Faith?

The fundamental fact of existence is that this trust
in God, this faith, is the firm foundation under
everything that makes life worth living.

(Hebrews 11:1)

Our God loves us deeply and longs to be in a relationship with us, His children. He yearns for us to receive the spiritual and physical blessings He is pleased to bestow upon His beloved children. Although we are followers, believers, imitators, and models of Jesus Christ, we will still suffer great loss. Our responses to these events can sometimes delay God's promises and purposes for our lives. Through the grief, pain, and pressure, we must be steadfast and immoveable in our faith by trusting in God to accomplish His purpose.

Enoch trusted God and that is why God took him away to heaven without dying. Noah trusted God. He believed God's warning about the future even though there were no signs of a flood and God saved him and his family. Abraham trusted God. God told him to leave home and go far away to another land—a land He promised to give him. Sarah, too, trusted God. In spite of her old age, she realized that God gave her a promise. A whole nation then came from Abraham and Sarah.

Before there can be purpose there must come pain. The magnitude of your pain is usually the measurement of your purpose. Do not fear your purpose. In Exodus 23:20-22, God said, "Now get yourselves ready.

I'm sending my Angel ahead of you to guard you in your travels, to lead you to place that I've prepared. Pay close attention to him. Obey him. Don't go against him. He won't put up with your rebellions because he's acting on my authority."

As you journey through the pages of this book, there will be opportunities to reflect on and record your own life experiences pertaining to grief and life's pressures. Gracefully pause for a moment to ponder these questions:

1. What if your godly purpose is meant to move mountains for many?

2. Why does death grab more attention than a purpose-filled life?

3. Are you afraid to die?

4. What if you journaled the things you don't want to leave unfinished?

5. How does grief affect your faith

So, what is faith? It is the confident assurance that something we have prayed for, according to His will, is going to happen. It is the certainty that what we hope for is waiting for us, even though we cannot see it up ahead. Our earnest, sincere prayer is our lifeline to God. Therefore, to activate our faith, we must earnestly pray and then trust God knows exactly what is best for us and for our loved ones.

In 2 Corinthians 5:7-8, it says, *"It's what we trust in, but don't yet see that keeps us going. Do you suppose a few ruts in the road or rocks in the path are going to stop us? When the time comes, we'll be plenty ready to exchange exile for homecoming."* Faith and trust go hand in hand. Therefore, we must trust God in all things no matter what we see happening around us. We must keep the faith even though the process may not feel good. He's working it out for our good and according to His purpose.

For God changes not and everything He spoke shall come to pass. He is able. His timing is perfect and He keeps all His appointments. One of God's most relevant promises to us as we face the challenges of life can be found in 2 Peter 1:3-8, where it says, "Everything that goes into a life of pleasing God has been miraculously given to us by getting to know, personally and intimately the One who invited us to God. The best invitation we ever received! We were also given absolutely terrific promises to pass on to you – your tickets to participation in the life of God after you turned your back on a world corrupted by lust. So don't lose a minute in building on what you've been given, complementing our basic faith with good character, spiritual understanding, alert discipline, passionate patience, reverent wonder, warm friendliness, and generous love, each dimension fitting into and developing the others. With these qualities active and growing in your lives, no grass will grow under your feet, no day will pass without its reward as you mature in your experience of our Master Jesus."

His divine power has given to us all things that pertain to life and godliness, through the knowledge of Him who called us by glory and virtue..." Then God tells us exactly how to be effective and productive in this life no matter what the world may throw at us. Oftentimes, I would remind myself by singing the lyrics of Helen Baylor's gospel song, titled, *If it Had Not Been*. The song begins with, *If it had not been for the Lord on my side*. Here is where I make it personal, He constantly wraps me in the cradle of His arms. So, if it had not been for the Lord on my side, I don't know where I would be.

CHAPTER ONE

Life

My Story

While at a family Christmas celebration in December of 2009, in the midst of joy, cheer, laughter, and the opening of Christmas gifts, I noticed my husband had lost a lot of weight. You live with a person, you see them dressed and undressed, you love them. Yet, for me, it wasn't until we had stepped out of our busy environment that my eyes opened to this revelation. There we were, a host of family members gathered around a beautiful Christmas tree, exchanging gifts, taking in the aroma of cinnamon and pumpkin spices, not to mention the ham and turkey that awaited us. When my husband, sitting next to me, cracked the place up with one of his jokes. Joining his laughter, I turned toward him. He had a laugh like none other. In fact, I first noticed its distinctiveness when we were dating. As he was still laughing, I turned to him and honed in on the extra space between his neck and shirt collar. It was a dead giveaway to something, but to what?

When we got back home after the holidays, still concerned, I addressed it with him. He tried to blow it off with a joke. He laughed, "What you mad because I'm losing weight, and you're trying?" I laughed, too, because that was a running joke we shared between us.

"No," I said, "You don't need to lose weight." Then as diplomatically as I could put it, while I wanted him to know that I meant business, I responded, "I'm making you an appointment for an early physical."

1

"Not now. I'm busy. I don't have time for a physical. Maybe later," he replied, half-joking, half-serious because he knew I was serious.

"Well, I'm making the appointment," I said, "and I will email you your itinerary, Mr. Busy Guy."

He relented and that was that. He reported to his initial doctor's appointment for his physical like a champ. A few days later, we received a phone call from his private doctor with instructions for him to have additional bloodwork completed. Here is where it all began. My husband had received the call on speaker, however, after the first order of instructions, my husband interrupted his doctor and announced he authorized all medical officials to speak directly to his wife. His doctor said, his request would be recorded in his medical file.

While still on speaker, we were advised the doctor's office had scheduled an appointment for a full-body CT scan, all he needed to do was show up. There I was diligently jotting down all that was being said, while keeping my thoughts under submission. After the call, I'm thinking, have I been given homework, yet not knowing the subject? It was time I accelerated to find out, what they saw that needed a full body CT scan to confirm. For the next two days, my husband continued his daily routines, business and life. On the other hand, I was tirelessly searching on the computer for the unknown. Believing I would find something, but fearful of what I'd find.

I am one who believes if you arrive on time, you're late. So, I usually arrive for my appointments an hour early. Of course, my husband reminded me over and over we were too early. Not so, when he was called in 20 minutes prior to his appointment.

As he prepared to walk back, I whispered, "Hey you, do you have something to say?"

He smiled and gave me a wink. I smiled back. After the scan, we were advised to go have lunch and come back in a couple of hours by a very nice, soft-spoken specialist. However, by no means could I eat. While we waited out the news of the unknown, I knew I was going to have to do whatever it took to encourage my husband, so I ate.

When we returned from lunch, we were called into a private room where the specialist went over the findings of the scan. There was a mass on his right kidney. A flood of questions circled the room. My husband stated he had no symptoms of any kind, or so he said. According to the specialist, a biopsy was not necessary. The result was Stage 3 cancer.

After receiving all the information there was to receive, my husband, triumphant once again, and went on with life. Even though our lives segued into sobering rounds of doctors' visits, medical tests, and antsy wait-times, we struggled to do our best to keep our lives as normal as possible. Later, further testing revealed the cancer had traveled through the small arteries into the lung. Surgery was pending to remove the right kidney, and a treatment plan was established. Through it all, during all the tests and prognoses, what I was really waiting for was for someone to tell me this was all a dream.

Only days after the diagnosis, I received a doctor's call at one o'clock in the morning asking me about my husband's daily routine and any concerns that I might have had.

"His right leg was dragging," I whispered into the phone. "His appetite has changed, and I am a little concerned."

There were other things I whispered into the phone that unexpected morning as I absorbed how intently the doctor had been listening. The doctor was so quiet, I wanted to ask him, "Are you still there?"

The doctor then spoke, "Wake up your husband and get him to the Washington Hospital Center, immediately, or have him transported by EMS."

His glucose was extremely high, and based on my report of his day, the doctor wanted to check him for signs of a stroke. I immediately called our son. He rushed over, and together, we drove him to the hospital. He was admitted immediately upon arrival. They knew we were coming. The doctors rushed to begin treatment and round-the-clock monitoring.

I had requested a private room and God made one available. Once settled in, I told my son he could leave.

"Dad and I are going to be okay," I assured him.

The hospital stay occurred over the weekend and the treatment was working extremely well. He was regaining his strength, his voice, and his appetite. My husband was even receiving and returning calls on his cell phone, conversing with every caller as if he was sitting in the comfort of his home. No one had any idea just where we were during those explosive few days except for our children. That Sunday, he was relaxed in the hospital recliner, chatting and laughing on the phone, and trash-talking about the football game. Before long, I had stretched across his hospital bed to catch a catnap.

We both were excited because, on the night before, we had been told he would be released sometime on Sunday. Preparing for a departure, we contacted our son and daughter to have them bring our vehicle to the hospital and park it in the hospital garage.

"You look really great," the doctor said. Cheerfully joking, he added, "Go home before we find something wrong with you." Then he said in a serious tone, "Follow the instructions provided and the scheduled surgery should go smoothly."

All this took place in January of 2010. The surgery was finally scheduled for late March. The doctor wanted to properly regulate his glucose.

When we arrived home, I felt an energy of peace and gratitude. Instinctively, my husband reclaimed the reins of our household. I watched him from our living room window as he walked the grounds and looked over the vehicles. I asked, "Lord, is this all a dream? Am I going to get one more phone call announcing this was all a mistake?" He looked so healthy to me. He had returned back to normal or so it seemed.

Month-after-month of follow-up doctor visits transpired; his medical condition had changed. Emergency surgery was scheduled for February of 2010. Prior to this surgery, they told us to get our family matters in order. So, I ran from doctor appointments, to meetings with our attorney, and then to getting documents notarized. At times, I felt like a train wreck on a wreck, but God was there with me even in the midst of all this chaos!

Key Points and Scriptures

In order to give you the utmost benefit from this book, my journey, I suggest that you pause at the end of each chapter to review the scriptures, questions, and key points. You can begin to reflect and keep a journal of those that directly minister to your specific situation in life. Allow God to bring you comfort and strength as you spend time with Him.

What does it mean to go *through* your difficult situation?

Romans 8:28; says, *"That's why we can be so sure that every detail in our lives of love for God is worked into something good."* Do you see how things are working out for your good?

During your time of bereavement, what did you learn about God and yourself?

Looking back over your life, have there been times when unusual and/ or challenging circumstances guided your life?

What does God promise you in 1 Peter 1:10-11?

Continue to pray. Ask God to open your eyes and your heart to what He has for you as you move forward through the pages of this book.

*"For we are newcomers at this, with a lot to learn, and
not too long to learn it."*

(Job 8:9)

*"Old people are distinguished by grandchildren; children
take pride in their parents."*

(Proverbs 17:6)

Life is a miracle, a gift given by God. A child is born. It's time to celebrate, to laugh, to rejoice, and sing praises to God for this precious gift of a child. Our parents rejoiced at our birth and then celebrated that birthdate every year thereafter. Yet, as we grow and mature into adulthood, we fail to seek the Creator and His purpose for our life. Jeremiah 1:5 says, "Before I shaped you in the womb, I knew all about you. Before you saw the light of day, I had holy plans for you." There will come a day when we have to give account of how we spent our lives.

God wrote a book about you and me. He's speaking to us every day about it. He has placed everything before us and nothing surprises Him. He wants to know that you and I know Him, His Son Jesus Christ, and that we know He has a plan and purpose for our lives. Every day is spent either working toward accomplishing His purpose or it is being wasted, but regardless, we shorten the distance to completing our time on Earth. God is always speaking to us through His Word, through others, and through our circumstances.

Are you attentive to His soft voice? How?

Have you ever asked God, what's His plan for you on this day?

_____

Have you ever talked with Him about your assignment?

_____

Who's influencing you?

_____

God designed life in stages from the newborn infant to the toddler. Then we move on to adolescent and teenager until we eventually reach adulthood and on through to our active senior years. We are taught by our parents how to be polite, patient, speak, and prepare for release into the world, or so we think. The truth of the matter is, God predestined our lives for His will, His pleasure, and His kingdom. He has designed each of our lives and given us all we need to accomplish His plan and purpose. In other words, God wants us to live our best *life*.

Here is where I was having a fight with God. I felt He had taken my husband too soon. But who was I to say that my husband's life was cut too short. What I did come to know was that it was not my call to make. God had the final say. No matter how it ended, my husband's life was a powerful legacy for our family, and for those who knew and loved him.

Life is a miracle. It can be long-lived for some, and short-lived for others. I encourage you all to live the best life possible and with gusto.

CHAPTER TWO

Love's Courtship

My Story

This tall cinnamon graduate, owning a confident smile, blocked the path to my locker. He called me by my name. I was a little startled by that, but I was not afraid because oddly enough I figured he knew my big brother. I knew, though, even back then, that my eyes betrayed my shyness; they always did. This handsome guy stood over me, all-up-in-my-face, and began to ask me a few questions which I answered with a monotoned, "No." *You've got a nerve*, I thought, since I had no idea who he was and had never seen him around my high school. I did think, however, he could have been from a neighboring school. Adding to all that surmising, he seemed very nice and extremely funny, but in that moment, I felt like I didn't have the time to get to know him. I was in a hurry. I had to get to cheerleading practice.

As the weeks went on, I thought, *This guy is persistent*. He showed up at every sports' event (home and away games), where he knew I would be cheerleading. On several occasions, particularly during school lunch hours, I spied him hanging out at the senior court. Yes, at this high school, being a senior was a big deal and it harbored many privileges. The seniors had a private courtyard located in the center of the school surrounded by huge glass windows. It was off limits to underclassmen. Because I soon came to notice his presence in the area, I began to ask a few questions of my own. Perhaps he was a senior or perhaps he had already graduated.

He knew my name before I knew his. Whenever I noticed him in the crowd, I made it a point to go the long way around to avoid him. I couldn't imagine, me a sophomore, coming home telling my parents a boy at school liked me, let alone someone who had already graduated from high school. I would become headless.

Two and a half months into the school year, we were approaching Homecoming Weekend. I was excited about the game, the dance, and hanging out with my classmates. My plan was to purchase my Homecoming ticket at the door. I hadn't bothered to check what my oldest brother and sister were going to do about tickets. The one thing I did know was we were set to ride together, so we had better come home together.

When we arrived at the school, I climbed out of the car, all excited, not paying much attention to my brother or sister. When I approached the door to purchase my ticket, a teacher and a police officer said, "No sales at the door. No ticket, no entry." There were many students in that predicament. I turned around looking for my brother and sister. They were still in the car. I hurried back to tell them I couldn't get in and my brother gave me this funny satisfied look.

I was thinking, *Why are you looking at me all crazy?* For some reason, he didn't seem concerned I couldn't get into the Homecoming dance. As it turned out, he had something up his sleeve, but I had missed it.

So, I exclaimed, "What on Earth am I going to do for the next three hours?"

My brother just gave me this relaxed look as he gazed, expectantly, beyond the hill, toward the entry to the school grounds. Powering over the hill were three popular hot-rods. Everyone knew those three cars and to whom they belonged. I knew instantly that my brother knew what was about to go down. His expression mutated into a confident smile. Well, the guy who had been watching and following me for the past few months was the driver of one of those hot-rods.

The guy, whom I had been intentionally trying to avoid, suddenly became my knight in shining armor that evening. He parked and walked over to where my brother and I were standing. They exchanged a few words before he asked me if I was going into the dance.

I answered a disappointed, "No."

Seeing him, my first assumption was I was being followed by him, once again. Unbeknownst to me, my admirer had respectfully approached my brother to arrange a formal meeting with me. In doing so, he was also asking for permission and my brother had given him the green light. Their original plan was to have us meet up during the Homecoming dance, but when that didn't work out, Plan B rolled right in without a hitch.

At my dear beloved husband's funeral, my brother took to the podium to recall when he had first met my husband. My brother told everyone that my husband was, "more than just a brother-in-law, he was my brother." He said, "We agreed on everything, except football teams." Everyone laughed. My brother shared comical details about the Homecoming dance so many years ago, including the fact they were Chevrolet men. That was a reference to the hot rods they drove. About arranging our meeting, my brother added how my new suitor, "had to pass my test [first]," because his sisters were special.

With my brother standing beside me in the school parking lot near the school gardens, which doubled as a social mecca for students, my admirer said, "Let's get something to eat."

I had been asking a few questions around the school about Mr. Confident. Everyone said he was so nice. He was so friendly, which boomeranged into a question to me, "Oh, you like him?" I neither confirmed nor denied.

"I'm just asking," was my standard reply. So, I must confess I wasn't that surprised to see him turn up at the dance or to notice how pleasant and kind he really was.

He took my hand, kissed it, and said, "It's going to be okay, let's go eat."

Back in those days, there were no eateries in the area. We had to travel to Oxon Hill, which was the next town over. We arrived at this carry-out place surrounded by other hot-rod drivers. It seemed as though he knew everyone. We grabbed a bite to eat, then stopped, laughed, and talked with nearly everyone. I was having a ball. I felt like Cinderella, who was getting something much better than a glass slipper. My admirer was slowly becoming the love of my life.

He held my hand the entire time that evening. It was comforting to me he was also mindful of my time that evening, after all, I wasn't where I was supposed to be—the dance. Considering the time, he looked at me with those forest brown, reflective eyes and suggested we had better head back to the school to meet up with my brother and sister. "I need to gas up, first," he said, which he did. As we pulled up to the school, we spotted my brother's car.

Before getting out of the car, I thanked him for everything, smiled, and said, "I enjoyed the dance."

He grabbed my hand, kissed it, and said, "Can I see you again?"

I smiled, and said, "I'll let you know."

Needless to say, I couldn't stop thinking about him for the rest of that fateful weekend. I was anxious to return back to school because I knew I would see him. However, before that could happen, I came down with a cold, and missed some days from school. By the time the next weekend rolled around, I was getting better, but I was still weak. On that Sunday, I was in my room, resting, when I heard what sounded like his vehicle coming down the street. Yes, I had already become accustomed to the unique sound of his hot rod. Panicked, I laid still to confirm what I thought I was hearing. I thought it was a dream; a dream I was having in my pajamas with my hair lumped and sweaty; not to mention owning a pair of puffy eyes and a runny red nose. Then I heard the front door bell. I said, "No, no, no, no, this is not happening." I could hear my heart pounding. There was nowhere to run and nowhere to hide for my dear life.

My mom called out my name and said, "Someone is at the door for you."

I thought, *Lord, have mercy on me. I know I'm dead. He's here at my house and my parents are going to freak out.* Rushing to pull myself together, which felt hopeless, I knew no one could have given him my address but my brother. *I'm gonna kill him*, I thought. What I was able to surmise, later, was that once my admirer had won approval from my brother, my brother then schooled him on how to win the approval of my parents. So, here he was, not only bearing gifts for them, but also the right gifts.

Slowly I got up and walked down the hall, thinking this cannot be happening. At the same time, I was looking for any one of my six siblings to stand as an eyewitness, hopeful they could stave off my execution. Also, I just knew my bold admirer was about to get chewed out or worse. Instead, I spied him giving my dad a six pack of Budweiser. That's right, my Dad was a die-hard Redskins fan and enjoyed the football games with a few Buds every Sunday. There was my mom, tickled as she walked away with her box of candy.

Before making my way to greet him, I remember slowly arriving at the thought, *I'm still alive. This must be okay.* Back then there were rules, restrictions, and huge road-block warnings to overcome if you wanted to get in good with a girl. Before that could happened, you had better get in good with her father.

After getting over the most critical hurdles, my parents allowed me to *date* him. I was so happy to have his company at school events, family picnics, holidays, etc. He would make me laugh so much, at times, it would hurt. He knew how to establish a pleasant environment and I looked forward to seeing him as often as I could. I liked him an awful lot and soon we became high school sweethearts. Sometimes life takes a turn when you least expect it. Yet, nothing just happens.

Unplanned, I became a mother before college, and had a family and a home before marriage. Nothing just happens. Everything happens for a reason. If I had life to do over, would I change anything? Absolutely! I would not have worried so much about the small things, especially about what others thought. Everyone said we were much too young to know anything about love, but we believed we were supposed to be together even though we realized we had done things out of order. One thing I knew for sure was God loved me. As I walked through this time with Him, I learned to rely on Him more and more.

Even when we make what looks like a mistake and/or detour off the path to our purpose, our God is in control and is always waiting to welcome His prodigal children back to His will.

Key Points and Scriptures

Are you living your purpose-filled life?

How so or why not?

Push your life's rewind button and take a moment to reflect and walk through the memories of your past. Go back as far as you can remember. You have an original, unique, and awesome story. Take a moment to reminisce.

What unique gifts or talents do you see God has given you in your life? How have you used these gifts?

I encourage you not to be troubled or embarrassed and don't allow others to convince you who you are to become. It's okay if you don't get it right on the first try—if you are booed off the stage. Get up, continue to seek and trust God, and use your God-given gifts. Has that happened to you? _____

Explain:

Don't accept their opinion about your identity or become a prisoner of someone else's view. The only thing that is important is what God says about you and live your best life.

What changes are you going to make in your life, now that you have reclaimed your life and strengthened your faith to know this truth and trust God?

Prayer: *So many choices and decisions seem to fill my world, Lord. I pray to rest in Your will and Your way so that I do not lose sight of my future as a person of God. My work can consume me, and my worries about little* *things can undermine the blessings. Change my heart, Lord. Let the matter of eternal importance become my priority. As I pray, a flood of securities fill me and make room for the purpose You wish to pour into my cup. Let me not be anxious to fill my life with clutter and trivial distractions, Lord. Let my life, my heart, and my soul be vessels that await the flow of Your Spirit. Show me how to use the gifts You have placed within me for Your glory and to fulfill Your purpose in my life.*

Don't panic. I'm with you. There's no need to fear for
I'm your God.
I'll give you strength. I'll help you. I'll hold
you steady
and keep a firm grip on you.

(Isaiah 41:10)

But the fact is, it was our pains he carried – our
disfigurements, all the things wrong with us. We
thought he brought it on himself, that God was
punishing him for his own failures. But it was our
sins that did that to him, that ripped and tore and
crushed him-our sins! He took the punishment, and
that made us whole. Through his bruises we get
healed. We're all like sheep who've wandered off and
gotten lost. We've all done our own thing, gone our
own way. And God has piled all our sins, everything
we've done wrong, on him.

(Isaiah 53:4-6)

Even when the way goes through Death Valley, I'm
not afraid when you walk at my side. Your trusty
shepherd's crook makes me feel secure.

(Psalm 23:4)

17

> *Light, space, zest – that's God! So, with Him on my side I'm fearless, afraid of no one and nothing.*

(Psalm 27:1)

CHAPTER THREE

Secret Inside the Secret

My Story

After many doctor visits and phone calls, emergency surgery was scheduled for February 2010 at 7:00 a. m., with a 5:00 a. m. arrival time for in-patient processing. I vividly recall it was an early Friday morning rise. Our usual mornings were upbeat and busy. While we both prepared for our workdays, we bustled around one another, getting dressed. The TV would be saying one thing, and the radio would be declaring something else. Daylight streaming into our bedroom was bright even if it rained. So, on this day, I knew I had to set the atmosphere. I had to keep it in the spirit and groove to which we were accustomed. I had to do it for his sanity and for mine. I had packed the night before, nonetheless, I was drilled by the patient. I mean, he was taking charge. He'd ask me if I had done this or that. He worked to keep us on schedule. He was absolutely ready to begin the steps to his recovery.

Before heading off, we prayed. Now, my husband was indeed a man of God, but he didn't like to pray out loud, but on that day he added a few words of his own. We loaded our luggage into the vehicle and drove off, knowing both of us were expecting to be at the hospital for at least three days. While slowly cruising passed our home, touched by its view, my unspoken words were, *Angels, in a few days we will be returning, in the meantime guard over our home from the north, south, east, and west. Please go to the hospital before us, inform the staff we are on our way. Sterilize the surgery room, equipment, instruments, hands, eyes, and minds.*

For surgery is about to take place on my precious cargo. Anytime is praying time and I love to pray!

The atmosphere was quite serene, calm, and pleasant. As we travelled to the hospital, fear was not welcomed, but lots of laughter was, as well as storytelling and instructions given by my husband. One may think that here was where things would have become difficult and our conversations would have turned to gloom and doom, but not so. When the presence of the Lord is with you, what keeps you going is His peace that surpasses all understanding.

We arrived at the Washington Hospital Center on time. We checked in and things began to move like clockwork. The staff was cheerful and very pleasant. A nurse entered our room to tell us the doctor had arrived and surgery would begin on time. She told my husband she was about to give him a few happy needles, and was there anything he wanted to say to her beforehand.

He said, "Yes. If you hurt me, I'm telling my wife."

There was a burst of laughter as if it was a set-up by the Lord. I walked with him alongside his bed as far as I could go. We journeyed in an elevator to a lower level and down several corridors on the way to the operating room. It was at these huge brown double doors that I could not go any further.

I tapped his nose and told him with a smile, "You are not the supervisor back there. And no flirting."

We laughed.

The nurse chimed in, "He better not or I going to tell his wife."

He was tickled.

Finally, I whispered to him, "I love you so much. I'll be here waiting with a kiss."

He took my hand, kissed it, and said, "I love you, too."

When he brought me home from our first date that infamous night of the homecoming dance, just before I got out of his car, he kissed my hand. Down through our years together, he would say to me, "Oh, these hands you've given me."

I was shown the way to the waiting room. It was cold. It was very early in the morning, so I pretty much had my choice of seats. To minimize even a second between the appearance of the three surgeons and what they had to tell me, I decided to sit next to the doors. I wanted to know the results of the surgery as soon as I could lay eyes on them. I had my water, my Bible, and the shortest prayer I knew, *Jesus, Jesus, Jesus*, along with a long wait ahead. While sitting alone, I would from time to time, whisper, "Lord, it's just you and I. Help me to control my thoughts and keep my crying to a minimum. You said You change not; well, neither has my prayer. Bring back my husband in good health."

The waiting room began to fill with the family members and friends of other patients. As I watched them await the news about their loved ones, tinges of envy and loneliness began to swarm around me. None of our family and friends were with me because my husband wanted to keep his illness a secret—at least, he thought, until he could get things under control. Lots of chatter and laughter was all around me, but none was for me. I started to second guess my strength. *Lord, will I be able to manage this all alone? How long will I be able to keep this up?*

I suddenly realized, with everything going on, I had forgotten to pray for myself. I was rattled and falling apart. *Lord, please don't let me pass out in this waiting room. Please fight and defeat the war of worry and fear on my behalf. As badly as I want to scream...somebody hold me and assure me that everything is already all right.*

Nine hours later, the doctors entered the waiting room and approached me with a smile. The lead surgeon announced that the surgery was a success. The second surgeon stepped up to say, "Please see to it that he maintains a good appetite." In those first moments, I was given a lot of information. The lead surgeon also told me he would be by that next day. The doctors informed me the nursing staff was to have my husband sitting up within the next forty-eight hours and have him walking within seventy-two hours. They said, if my husband was a good patient, he should be released to go home within four-to-five days.

I asked, "When can I see him?"

One of the doctors gave a compassionate smile and said, "Now. Follow me."

All of them escorted me back to the recovery room.

Still heavily sedated, he was calling my name almost before I reached his side. Even though he was woozy, he was probably taking in my perfume. With the doctors leading the way, I tried to rush by, but had to announce from afar, "I'm here. Everything is okay, I'm here."

All this was said before I could wholly see him, but once I was there and grabbed his hand, he quiet down. He tightly gripped my hand at the knowledge of my presence and I could feel his energy telling me, I'm not never letting go. I felt the same. A heaviness had been lifted off my shoulders even though I knew it was going to be a long road ahead to recovery.

The stay in the hospital proved to be a total of four days. We both were very thankful to be heading home together. We knew we were about to go on a journey which would be the beginning of an aggressive treatment plan.

We were in the car, I was driving, and with confident definition, he said, "Let's get in position for the mission."

Not only was the ride home full of instructions, but life seemed to be still full of promises. Unlike the look I spied on him, four months ago when I detected the space between his neck and shirt collar, on this day, my husband looked pleasantly healthy. His complexion had returned to its rich cinnamon glow. Although, he had been through a major surgery, there appeared to be no evidence on his face or body. He didn't believe it was a good idea to tell our son and daughter what was going on because he didn't want to alarm them and he believed that things were going to get better. At this stage, things had begun to look very hopeful.

In May of 2010, he was released back to light duty. My husband didn't like the idea of light duty. He thought he was Batman, Superman, and Spiderman; he certainly was my hero. He kicked up so much fuss, by early June of 2010, he managed to get his way and return to his regular schedule. His doctors allowed us both to return to our respective offices. While treatment and care continued, he was happy and excited, and believed he had turned an important corner. He endured his daily chemo medication, while I administered his daily diabetic shots. The hospital staff had trained me before he was discharged. Zeroing in on his appetite, I prepared home-cooked meals every day—breakfast, lunch, and dinner. I got up early every morning to prepare his breakfast and lunch before leaving for the office, and dinner was served every evening. There was no eating out.

Our prayers had been answered. Praying and worshiping God for life. His remission had inspired us to resume to our normal lives. While recuperating and gaining back his strength, he quickly resumed driving his hot rod, mowing the lawn, washing his vehicles, and getting back to other various daily activities. While home together, I never let him out of my sight. Looking through every window, from every view at every angle, I knew where he was at all times. We even started back to our long walks. We enjoyed walking, talking, and watching the cars go by.

He was doing so well until September of 2010. We both took notice of a change in his walking and appetite. I would kid with him about trashing my lunch and eating out with colleagues and having a huge lunch. Of course, he would refuse to admit it. While still going to work, one evening we arrived home simultaneously. That was almost impossible for us to do because we worked on opposite sides of town. After parking my vehicle, I looked over at him, thinking to myself, *why is he still in his work truck*? I placed my bags back into my vehicle and walked over to his.

I called his name, he answered, and I asked, "Are you on the phone?"

He responded, "No."

I asked, "Are you okay, ready to get out?"

He said, "Yes."

He wasn't moving on his own strength. So, I opened the door, grabbed his arm and said, "I got you."

He didn't want to agree he needed help, and said, "My leg went to sleep."

Trying to avoid saying anything about his health or upset him in anyway, I replied, "Let's wake it up, and get you in the house."

He was still going to work, but slowing down. In the progression of that, I adjusted my office hours so that I could be there to help him tie his tie or button his shirt. I wasn't feeling good about the changes in his condition. So, I contacted the doctor to request appetite enhancers and shared all my concerns about the latest turn of events. The doctor wanted him to come in prior to his next appointment.

Keeping with the appointment and having been there for what seemed like all day, both doctors finally entered into the room and began to explain how the cancer had spread into several places aggressively. One doctor suggested we take a cruise or go on a long vacation. Both the diagnosis and advice were not received in a friendly way by my husband. I looked over at my husband, still having authority over his thoughts and belief.

He responded, "A cruise is out of the question! I'm a keep-my-feet-on-the-ground guy. Besides, we are on vacation every day. So, what's next?"

The doctors explained more to us, and recommended hospice to assist me, since my husband would need more and more care in the days to come. I welcomed the medical services, but insisted that his personal care, I would manage.

Key Points and Scriptures

The nights of crying your eyes out give way to days of laughter.

(Psalm 30:5)

The loss of a loved one is not easy. Whether or not it is due to sickness, a criminal act, or if it is accidental, the suffering is quite overwhelming. We try to *soldier on*, shrugging it off, and push to get back to business as quickly as possible.

Why do we feel we have to do that?

Who are we doing it for?

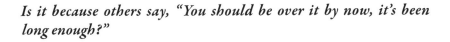

Is it because others say, "You should be over it by now, it's been long enough?"

Is it because they tell us, "It's time to get back into the flow of life?

However, it is not realistic to think that professing to have the answers to these questions is all you have to do. The reality is, a personal loss shakes you, saps your strength, and leaves you in a billion pieces. You feel pain in places you didn't know you had. Yes, even for people of faith, it still hurts. We still suffer denial, anger, depression, and a shutdown to the point of wanting to close out the world and cry out, "Why, Lord, why?"

No matter who we are, we all experience the whole spectrum of human emotion. If you are reeling from the loss of a loved one, realize it's normal. If you find yourself crying all night, sleeping all day, or suddenly doing strange things, don't fret. It doesn't mean you're going crazy. It just means you've lost someone you really loved. There is no surefire formula and no pill that will magically cure you of your grief. Time helps, but faith heals! The support of family and solid friends will get you through the worst of it. However, it is important to realize you have to go through and overcome the grief, pain, and the pressure to get to

God's purpose for your life. God's plan for you does not end when you experience the loss of a loved one.

There will always be a tender spot in your heart, a corner dedicated to the memory of the one you've lost. You might get back to normal in a year or so, but you'll still shed an occasional tear. That is as it will be. There will be times when you will need a deeper comfort. When that happens, you certainly don't want to be told, "Don't feel bad." Because, now, you don't want to feel bad about feeling bad. Feeling bad about losing a loved one just might be your normal state of life for quite some time. People want to show their concern for you, and if you're strong enough, you want to acknowledge that these consolations are lovely gifts. Having said that, you also need to hear God has not forgotten you and He will embrace you in the most difficult times.

You need to be reassured you will get through the pain. However, you also need to understand there is no way around it. You have to go through it, but rest assured, a new day will dawn at the end of this dark night of the soul. You need to hear that your muddled feelings, hollering, and throwing things will not make you a weak believer or a bad person. The loss of a loved one affects your entire self, mind, emotions, body, and spirit. Know this, the grieving process begins whenever it needs to and continues as long as it has to.

It's even possible that after hearing the gloomy prognosis of a terminal illness, the grieving begins at the anticipation of death, like it did for me. Uncertainty can definitely begin the whole grieving process, even if you don't want it to show.

CHAPTER FOUR

The Breaking of Secrets

My Story

After the visit by hospice, the following day was his birthday. My husband told me he was ready to tell our son and daughter and he wanted to do it individually and by himself. I never questioned him, but I wanted to ask, "Are you sure? On your birthday?" I just couldn't muster up the strength to push the words out of my mouth or to even suggest, "How about another time?" I was thinking *the longer he put it off, the longer we will have him*. Later, I realized, he had something he wanted to tell them both, and to give them an opportunity to express their feelings without anyone else being involved. Struggling with my own thoughts, I decided it would be best to stay busy.

He actually called me in the room and asked with a smile, "Why don't you slow down? Take a break, you're making me dizzy."

Holding on with a few secrets of my own, I thought that I was going to lose my mind. When he told me to sit down next to him and listen closely.

He went on to say, "I've been meaning to speak with you, but could never catch you. I want you to slow down and relax. You and I both know I am not going to be here much longer."

I gave him that look that said, "Don't say that."

He said firmly, "Yes, this is true. And so, two things, please, I want to be home. Hospitals are too cold, and there's no place like home. Also, it's time I ask for your forgiveness."

I gave him another confused look, thinking, *You want my forgiveness? Why?*

He said, "I am sorry to leave you this way. I don't want to go, and I can't take you with me, but I believe in my heart you will be just fine. It doesn't seem to be so right now, but give it some time. Remember me always, and I promise to remember you longer. You are an amazing, strong, impressive, and full of surprises wife. Thank you for choosing me and being the mother of my children. You made every day exciting. You courageously built up this family in leaps and bounds and never disappointed me. You are so intelligent, gifted with a mental power to always accomplish what you set out to do. I used to study you, not for control, but to understand how you manage."

Because his illness had taken such a toll on his energies, I could see him working to give me a smile as he continued, "I learned your secret and it is safe with me."

I smiled back, listening to every word.

My husband went on, "Even when we would disagree, I knew eventually I was going to give in and let you have your way. It ended up, most of the time you knew best. On all occasions you always knew how to bring out the best in me. In time, and only when you're ready, you will need to prepare yourself to love again."

I just couldn't imagine loving again, but I kept silent.

"When the right guy shows up, and he will show up, you will know. He's going to offer you something different than what I gave you, give him a chance. He will know early on what a smart, gifted, and beautiful woman you are, so go ahead and love again."

I noticed that he was becoming tired, but he insisted I call our son over to the house. I arose from my chair to quickly leave the room to do so. I felt as though I was suffocating and needed to clear the distance between us.

I quickly went downstairs, fell across the sofa, bowed on my knees, and called on the Lord, "Lord, here I am on bended knees pleading to You. I am not ready to die. I feel like I'm losing and falling apart. I refuse to give my pain authority to kill me. The troubles of my heart are enlarged, help me. Lord please, help me. You said You will never put more on me than I can bear. My load is getting heavy, and I don't know what more to say. I'm out of words, running out of strength.

Lord don't let me collapse now, my husband needs me." All I could do was place my face in a pillow and cry out, "Why, Lord? Why?" In the midst of my brokenness, I realized I had better pull it together and call our son.

When our son arrived, he greeted me with a pleasant smile and a hug as usual and asked, "Where's Dad?"

I replied, "Upstairs. He'll be happy to see you."

I didn't go upstairs with him, I thought it would be best to leave them alone, so I decided to leave the house to take a drive for some fresh air. A few hours later, I called home; no answer. I immediately began to cry out, "I will trust in the Lord with all my heart and lean not unto my own understanding!" (Proverbs 3:5). My hands and legs became very weak; I began to shake and cry more.

While travelling on Highway 301 South, a text came through, it was my son. Before actually reading his message, I assumed he was telling me to come home. Instead, it was a picture of my son's hand tightly interlocked with his father's hand. The text message beneath the photo read, "keeping a piece of my dad." I quickly called his number, my son answered by accepting the call, but was silent. There was no hello. I called his name, and he started to cry, and so did I. At this time, I was paused at a traffic light that had now turned green. I was paralyzed there, still crying. I could not see anything. Everything was a blur, which prevented me from proceeding. I started to struggle with searching for the hazard lights and the buttons to let my windows down for air. Motorists did their best to go around as I rushed to get it together for the next green light. I gripped the steering wheel and cried out, "Lord help me, my destination is home. Please carry me in."

I arrived home safely, placed the vehicle in park, and said, "Thank you, Jesus. I need You, Lord, come in, stay, order my footsteps and direct my path." I approached the bedroom, my son and his dad were both there sleeping peacefully, nestled next to one another. I went to a quiet room, turned my face to the wall, and prayed unto the Lord.

The following day, I reached out to our daughter. She returned my call to say she was on her way. She asked if I wanted anything like she normally does. I responded with a, "No thank you, my love," and quickly asked about the kids. Conversations about the grandkids would always make a happy mood. Then I made excuse to jump off the phone to prevent her from asking questions about her father.

When she arrived, even though I tried to hide my pain, she instantly picked up on it, and asked, "It's really bad isn't it?"

Even though their dad wished not to burden them, I believed in my heart they had noticed the many changes in his lifestyle.

She went on to say her husband said, "Please don't come back home with bad news."

When I asked if she wanted some time alone, she grabbed my hand and we walked up the stairs together. The moment she entered the room, she fell into her father's arms and they both wept. There were moments of crying followed by stilled quietness. I knew to leave the room, to give them some time together, but I chose not to leave the house. Yes, my daughter is a beautiful woman, mother, and wife, she will forever be my baby-girl. I knew she wanted me near.

On November 1, 2010, a day before our wedding anniversary, I had been jetting around the house, doing anything and everything, but most importantly, keeping my husband comfortable. I read the paper to him, I took him up on suggestions for lunch, dinner, and a snack, while still discussing household matters.

Hours later, my husband called out my name in a soft-spoken voice and said, "Come in here, rest, take a break. No, take a nap with me."

I thought, *that seems like a great idea*, so I did.

He turned toward me and whispered in my ear, "Whatever happens, I want to be home."

I smiled and said, "Yes Sir!" I thought, We've been over this before. Later, I found myself asking, was that his goodbye?

Awakening from a much-needed nap, it was late in the evening and dark outside, as well as in the room. I reached over to turn on the lights, looked over at my husband. His eyes were tightly shut, he was still as a statue, frozen into place, and he looked non-responsive. I thought he was dead until I noticed he was struggling with his breathing. He was panting.

We had been offered hospice care, and though I declined the personal care, I agreed to the minimum monitoring. They advised that when his condition worsened do not call 911, but call them. I did and someone arrived within minutes. They brought in an oxygen tank and performed a thorough examination. My son and daughter arrived. It was explained to us that my husband may not make it through the weekend, less than 72 hours. The hospice care nurse asked if I knew the signs of death. My mind was circling around the room and I couldn't make it stop.

Have you ever had someone hold you down with a pillow over your face and you're fighting for air? Well that was what I felt at that moment.

I overheard the nurse asking my daughter, "Will your mom be okay?"

My daughter responded, "Yes, just give us a moment."

The hospice care nurse was there for over an hour. Everyone was doing what was needed to make my husband as comfortable as possible. From that day forward, I functioned only by God-given strength. I bathed, dressed, sang, talked, exercised, and administered my husband's medication. Keeping my eyes on him at all times, around the clock. I was not going to have my husband leave and not be by his side. I kept asking myself what really went on during that long nap.

On November 5, 2010, I watched my husband transition over and take his final breath. I walked around to his bedside, embraced him, and whispered, "I love you, and I'm going to miss you so much." I continued to hold him and sobbed. Remembering the orders given by the hospice care nurse, I called the nurse to give her the sad news.

The hospice care nurse arrived at my house in minutes, and shortly thereafter the coroner. I had asked her to give me a minute. I needed some time to dress my husband in his favorite jogging suit before I allowed him to be taken away. My son and daughter helped me.

Then the nurse came back into the room, asking, "Are we ready?"

Following her in the room was the coroner pushing a long stretcher. I looked over at the gentleman and watched him as he unfolded a large black bag.

I stumbled my way through everyone, saying, "Excuse me, please excuse me."

I couldn't stomach what was about to take place next, so I ran into the office nearby.

Our daughter followed behind me and asked, "Mom, are you okay?"

I continued to shake my head back and forth, "No."

Then the nurse came in and asked the same question, "Are you okay?"

Lost for words, I gave her a gloomy stare. She nodded her head, left the room, but quickly returned. She informed me the coroner would not close the bag, but would leave his face exposed hopeful for a better departure. I was still at a loss for words. The nurse understood, and on my behalf, granted the coroner permission to pass through. Instinctively, she knew I was in no condition to take part or watch. It was on that night, my husband's journey had ended, while mine had just taken a detour.

Key Points and Scriptures

God knows when we will lose a love one and will eventually have to face the truth we will be taking the rest of our life's journey without them. He is aware we will begin to feel a deep loneliness and then fear. So, when a winter of loneliness comes, whisper to your Father in prayer.

"Heavenly Father, I know You didn't promise days without pain,
Laughter without sorrow, nor sun without rain,
But You did promise strength for our days,
Comfort for the tears, and light for the way
And under your wings shall I trust."

Denial and Anger

Denial is generally the first step of the grieving process. Losing a loved one just does not seem real at first. Anger is then the next step. Though it does not seem like it at the time, anger actually begins to move us toward healing when it is allowed to be expressed. It is an emotional response that definitely needs to be expressed outwardly and not trapped inside. The deep anger so many may have about losing a loved one is there seems to be no life line to grab hold of. Without an egress to release it through, anger builds up like steam in a pressure cooker and will eventually explode. The little bird of faith is likely to get its tail feathers singed in the process. So how do we learn to recognize and allow that anger to be expressed in a healthy way?

Family, friends, pastors, and others will try to be there for us. They all mean well, however, there's nothing one can say to make the pain go away. People will speak words of comfort, but unless they understand the grieving process, they may not help us move forward toward healing. Sometimes, we just need to separate ourselves from well-meaning family and friends and seek time with the Lord.

Our anger can be rooted in what I refer to as the "why war." We are not falling apart at this point, but we are angry. Thank God, He gives up permission to cry, scream, get angry, and ask why. "Go ahead," He says, "I am still God on the throne and have everything you need."

He is not offended as we vent and share with Him the surge of emotions we are experiencing inside. In fact, He wants us to come to Him so we can receive the healing we need to move us forward in the process toward His purpose.

As you seek God's guidance, know that you are not alone in the world either. There are others grieving from their loss and they are going through the same process. There are multiple support groups that consist of people who truly do know what you are going through because they have been through it themselves. They can often be of more help to you than friends and family. They will not be offended when you share your true feelings.

While some may want to withdraw from the crowd, others will put on a strong face to seem like they have it all together. The truth is, no matter what it looks like on the outside, inwardly, a person who is struggling with grief may need to try and sort through his or her feelings privately. People need the comfort of relationships, but they also need that alone time where they do not have to put on a "together" face. There will be moments when we will kick and scream simply because we are emotional beings. These are the times we need a safe place where we do not damage other relationships, while we process through our grief.

Holding onto Hope in the Midst of the Storm

*So, we're not giving up. How could we! Even though on
the outside it often looks like things are falling apart on*

33

us, on the inside, where God is making new life, not a
day goes by without his unfolding grace.

(2 Corinthians 4:16)

There will be times when we're going to question, how does one stand on the Word of God when hope seems abandoned and faith is hemorrhaging? When we lose someone precious, it's an emotional issue and quickly becomes a spiritual challenge. We tend to feel God has betrayed us and that creates another major loss in our lives. It is a loss of intimacy with our Creator, perhaps even a loss of faith. I personally dealt with this by making a determined effort to spend time with God before closing my eyes at night and prior to planting my feet on the floor in the morning. I would send up a prayer for God's safety and protection to cover me as I walked through the grieving process. I knew that I needed to have that relationship or I would not make it through.

Of course, we try to avoid it at first. We attempt various tactics to keep from confronting and even try to avoid the full force of the loss. We focus on our work or our faith. We passionately adopt a positive mental outlook. We throw ourselves into activities of various sorts. Denial seldom actually rejects the reality of the loss, though there might be daydreams and wistful moments when we temporarily forget the loved one has passed. Eventually though, we have to move forward and journey through the pain, the pressure, and the process to get to His purpose.

Key Points and Scriptures

So, how does one stand on the Word of God when hope seems abandoned and faith is hemorrhaging?

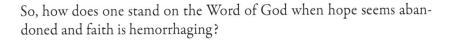

It is important to realize you have to *Go Through and Overcome the Grief, Pain, and Pressure, to Reclaim Your Purpose* for your life.

How has this revelation helped you in moving forward through the grieving process in your life?

Also realize, God is not offended as we vent and share with Him the surge of emotions we are experiencing inside. In fact, He wants us to come to Him so we can receive the healing we need to move us forward in the process toward His purpose.

How has this revelation helped you in moving forward through the grieving process in your life?

There are multiple support groups that consist of people who truly do know what you are going through because they have been through it themselves. They can often be of more help to you than friends and family. They will not be offended when you share your true feelings. Here are a few websites you can search through to find help and support in your area.

www. Betterhelp.com

www. LocalGuides.com

www. Griefshare.org

www. Hospicefoundation.org/.../Support-Groups

Prayer: *Father God, I ask that You give me the warmth of Your presence. I need Your help with understanding that loneliness will bring me closer to You. Hear my cry, home is lonely, but I trust and believe in Your promises to make my heart Your home. I know You are with me always. Thank You for being there for me.*

> *The Spirit of God, the Master, is on me because God anointed me. He sent me to preach good news to the poor, heal the heartbroken, announce freedom to all captives, pardon all prisoners. God sent me to announce the year of his grace – a celebration of God's destruction of our enemies – and to comfort all who mourn, to care for the needs of all who mourn in Zion, give them bouquets of roses instead of aches. Messages of joy instead of news of doom, a praising heart instead of a languid spirit. Rename them "Oaks of Righteousness" planted by God to display his glory.*
>
> (Isaiah 61:1-3)

CHAPTER FIVE

Pain and Pressure on Display

My Story

Broken, sad, angry and interrupted by this voice that was constantly telling me to recalculate. I refused to sit in church, in the presence of happy saints, coupled with their spouses. There I was home sitting under my mountain. I had no plans on opening the blinds, answering the phone and/or the door. As the days and nights would pass me by, I had no sense of direction. I attempted from time-to-time to watch a television ministry program, and while doing so, at no time was I truly engaged in the program. Still, I overheard a preacher speaking about giving God glory the minute you open your eyes in the morning. It was His grace that kept you alive, he sputtered, above ground and not in the grave. *Really?* I thought to myself, Explain that to the grieving widow and her children.

Maybe you're thinking I am being extremely disrespectful and ungrateful to the Lord. Absolutely not! Because of my brokenness, I am being everything He had given me permission to be; angry, hurt, mad, and even the permission to question Him. Why? As the preacher continued to speak, his words just made it seem all the more unfair. I felt robbed. Death invaded my marriage and snatched my husband away from me.

I reminded the Lord, "I gave You my true heart. While praying and believing for healing for others, I needed to know why didn't that same wonderous working power work for my husband?" I continued to ask, "Why didn't You prevent this, Father? You took my husband away too soon. Here I am left holding our unfulfilled plans. What am I to do now?"

I want to strongly express, you are not yourself. It may appear as though your fights with God are somewhat harsh and a little rude, but our God knows us better than we know ourselves. He knew what I was thinking and would do before it even happened. He knew I would be up all through the night, fighting and crying out loud, letting Him know that I'm sad, I'm hurting, I'm angry, and I have nothing to say right now.

So, go ahead, let it out. Where you are weak, God wants to come to make you strong.

Key Points and Scriptures

"In sickness and in health, until death do us part," we speak these words to one another as we enter into marriage. We are the designers of our vision. We write the vision for a happily-ever-after marriage and we plan to grow old together. We see the perfect mate, family, job, house with a white picket fence, and living a life of joy, abundance, and success. We write the guest list, choose the location of the church, pick out our favorite flowers, select the colors, and so on as we plan to begin our lives together. Nowhere in the vision do we see death, even though we speak those words within our vows. The thought is usually not there on that day of wedded bliss. It is not something you want to focus on or even think about on your wedding day. It's like by denying it, it will never happen to our marriage.

When death invades our vision, the pain we carry can be staggering, and it may leave us feeling hopeless, helpless, and struggling with trying to cope with what this means as we attempt to continue our life's journey. While the pain may never go away, it does lessen with time. However, it is important to realize grief does not have a timeline. Don't let well-meaning friends and family try to tell you when you should be over each stage of the grieving process.

Crying can be a way of releasing frustration and overwhelming pain so you can move forward and face the day. You will find you will feel much better after a good cry. Tears are a natural part of our emotional cleansing system and they promote our ability to heal. I found that my tears were and still are a part of my strength. If I need to find a place to be alone to sit in God's lap and cry for a while, I do it. He wraps His arms of love around me and just lets me pour my heart out to Him.

Soon and very soon, you will find yourself praising the Lord even in the midst of your storm. He promised to never leave us nor forsake us. Go ahead, be at home with the Lord.

The Blame Game

The next level of grief is usually the blame game. That is what I was doing. When we are hurting or feeling abandoned, we need to blame and lash out at someone or something. Eventually, we get around to being angry with God. The "whys" will progress to, "Why didn't You prevent this from happening, God?" What we are doing is blaming God for not intervening on behalf of the loved one we have lost.

Don't misunderstand me. We know the devil is out to attack marriages and families, but we often do not realize if our anger and blame are not properly handled, we can open the door, allowing the enemy to try to draw us away from God—our true source of healing. A thief is only there to steal and kill and destroy (John 10:10). Don't allow the enemy to tempt you to hibernate in your pain. Don't move away from God. Don't let the devil steal your joy, hope, and happiness. Move toward God. Put on the armor of God as it will give you the strength to withstand the fight.

Be prepared. You're up against far more than you can handle on your own. Take all the help you can get, every weapon God has issued, so that when it's all over but the shouting you'll still be on your feet.

(Ephesians 6:13)

39

The armor of God consists of the helmet of salvation, breastplate of righteousness, sword of the spirit, shield of faith, and boots to walk through the valley of the shadow of death until you achieve the peace only God can give you. Then remember there's power in your words. What you consistently say, whether good or bad, will have a great impact on your life. That's why it's so necessary to speak words of healing to allow the healing process to begin. You need to use what God has placed in your hand, which is the sword of the spirit to cut away the pain, heartaches, headaches, backaches, etc.

Proverbs 18:21 says, "Words kill, words give life; they're either poison or fruit – you choose."

So take control of the words that you speak over your life. In fact, Jesus tells us in Matthew 7:7, "Don't bargain with God. Be direct. Ask for what you need. This isn't a cat-and-mouse, hide-and-seek game we're in."

> *I don't think the way you think. The way you work isn't the way I work." God's Decree. For as the sky soars high above earth, so the way I work surpasses the way you work, and the way I think is beyond the way you think.*

> (Isaiah 55:8-9)

Remember, Joseph replied, "*Don't be afraid. Do I act for God? Don't you see, you planned evil against me but God used those same plans for my good, as you see all around you right now – life for many people*" (Genesis 50:20). God's timing is always perfect. His ways are not our ways, so when we trust in His ways, He walks us through to His perfect peace. Our thoughts about life tend to miss the things of true value such as life, family, health, sound mind, friendships, etc. Don't let the unknown timeline after the loss of a loved one hold you back from what is really important in life as you move forward and walk with God through to the other side of grief.

*I'm telling you these things while I'm still living with
you. The Friend, the Holy Spirit whom the Father will
send at my request, will make everything plain to you.
He will remind you of all things I have told you. I'm
leaving you well and whole. That's my parting gift to
you. Peace. I don't leave you the way you're used to being
left – feeling abandoned, bereft. So don't be upset. Don't
be distraught.*

(John 14:25-27)

Depression is quite often the next phase of our grieving process. Being depressed is not being crazy. We all experience depression from time to time, it's almost a fact of life. When there's too much stress in our lives we get overwhelmed and when we're overwhelmed our emotional responses shut down. The clinical definition of depression says it is a mood disorder, which means our emotional mood is or has been down for a period of time. I was able to move through my period of depression without professional help. However, I highly recommend seeking professional help if the depressed mood lasts for more than thirty days.

One of the most powerful strategies Jesus used to defeat Satan and live His life in 100 percent victory was knowing there was no possibility for defeat. The night before He was crucified, Jesus knew His hour had come. He knew the time appointed when He would leave the Earth and return to His Father had come. Jesus also knew God was in control of His circumstances. He knew His life was not in the hands of the Jews or the Pharisees or Pilate, but in the hands of His Father. Jesus did not look forward to His death just as we do not look forward to the death of a loved one. However, He did not view it as defeat, but rather victory.

We cannot view it as a defeat, but as a time of great victory. Jesus told His disciples earlier, "Listen carefully: Unless a grain of wheat is buried in the ground, dead to the world, it is never any more than a grain of wheat. But if it is buried, it sprouts and reproduces itself many times over. In the same way, anyone who holds on to life just as it is destroys that life. But if you let go, reckless in your love, you'll have it forever, real and eternal" (John 12:24-25). Jesus knew He must face the pain and suffering of the cross knowing that through His death, He would bring glory and honor to our Father and make salvation available to all mankind.

We have to go through the floods of emotion and endure the pressure and the pain. We can go through the process without worrying or wondering what's going to take place next because of what Jesus did on the cross for us. Jesus even gave us an example of how to attain our victory.

> *Keep your eyes on Jesus, who both began and finished this race we're in. Study how he did it. Because he never lost sight of where he was headed – that exhilarating finish in and with God – he could put up with anything along the way: Cross, shame, whatever. And now he's there, in the place of honor, right alongside God. When you find yourselves flagging in your faith, go over that story again, item by item, that long litany of hostility he plowed through. That will shoot adrenaline into your souls!*

(Hebrews 12:2-10)

Jesus was able to endure the stripes on His back and the pain on the cross because He knew God had given Him all power and authority to achieve the victory. Just know that during the process you will face broken-heartedness, depression, worry, sadness, anxiety, and loneliness, but you have all the power of our Lord and Savior backing you up to walk you through the rains of adversity and the floodtides of doubt and despair. At the time, you may ask, will it ever get better? Being a Christian and trusting in His Word doesn't make us immune to the storms of life. However, it does mean He is right there with us every step of the way. Jesus will bring us through this flood, through the storm, and He will get us to the other side.

Key Points and Scriptures

Proverbs 18:21 says, "Words kill, words give life; they're either poison or fruit – you choose." This means you need to take control of the words you speak over your life.

What words are you using to describe your life?

Do you have any words and phrases you may need to change? If so, take a moment to list them.

In John 14:27, Jesus said, "*I'm leaving you well and whole. That's my parting gift to you. Peace. I don't leave you the way you're used to being left – feeling abandoned, bereft. So don't be upset. Don't be distraught.*"
How has this promise from Jesus helped you as you move along your journey to healing?

Look at the example Jesus left us as He endured painful journey to the cross.

What did He know about God that helped Him complete His mission and attain the victory?

What do you know about God that is helping you to attain the victory as you walk through your storm?

What is the answer to the storms of life, the swirling winds, the torrential life, particularly when it involves the imminent death of a loved one?

Prayer: *Father God, please help me turn to You for guidance and strength as I go through the storms of life. Thank You for the peace that You give even in the midst of the storm. I put my trust in You for I know You will guide me every step of the way. Thank you, Lord for the strength and help You give me.*

Just like in the song, written by Joseph M. Scriven, titled, "What a friend we have in Jesus. Yes, it is a privilege to carry everything to God in prayer!"

CHAPTER SIX

Healing Process on The Way

My Story

What is the answer to the storms of life, the swirling winds, the torrential life, particularly when it involves the imminent death of a loved one?

One of the worst storms for me was watching my beloved husband's health deteriorate knowing there was nothing I could do about it. That's when the full reality of my impending loss came crashing down on me. I was forced to accept the truth and to let the sadness hit. I got weepy, lethargic, couldn't taste my food, and didn't care about the things I used to enjoy. I didn't sleep well. I went through my days in a haze. I found I needed to spend time with the Lord dealing with the truth. The only way out of the pain was to walk through it with my friend Jesus by my side.

It's not easy dealing with or properly preparing for the coming death of a loved one. Another dynamic in this experience is that dying people need to be understood. In the case of a terminally-ill loved one, sometimes their family members become so overwhelmed by their own emotions they forget that their loved one is still in need of encouragement and companionship. They may continue to give instructions and orders to fight the fear of the enviable. We must allow them the freedom to make their preparations their way as much as possible.

My husband repeated to me, "I don't ever want to be a burden. I will let you know what I need and when, but until then I got this." He always tried to stay on top of the situation and not to let the illness get to him or weigh him down. He never wanted to relinquish control or give me the impression he had given up. He made me promise to allow him to tell our son and daughter in his way and in his time. He did not want me to tell anyone else about the extent of his illness until there was nothing left he could do.

In the weeks following his requests, I found even more to worry about. I had to care for my husband in secrecy. I was afraid and angry.

Key Points and Scriptures

I've been in the floodtides of sorrow. As the rains and winds beat upon my life and the floods tried to overwhelm me, I held on to the Lord, my rock, my fortress, and my deliverer (Psalm 18:2). Not everyone responds in exactly the same way to hard times in their personal lives. However, we don't have to be discouraged or depressed because Jesus promised that He will never leave us nor forsake us—no matter what we are going through.

Keep your head up above the floodwaters by remembering you have a lifeline directly to the Lord. You don't need manufactured prayers when you've been through something. You will have your own custom-built, personal prayer when you share with God from your heart to His heart, from your lips to His ears.

God hears your prayers. I will admit it may be difficult to step back from your emotions during trying circumstances, but that is what you have to do to function properly. You can't let yourself be tied in knots, losing the ability to function. You do not have to be paralyzed by the storms of life. Jesus said that if you build your life on Him, the solid rock, the storms cannot prevail against you. With Jesus by your side, you can make it through the storm.

Where is God when we need Him?

At first, I felt abandoned in my time of great need. However, the truth is, God was right there with me all the way. Though I did not recognize Him right away, He was always close at-hand. He allowed me to move out on my own a little, but He was never far away. "Do Not Fear," the Lord said, "Don't panic. I'm with you. There's no need to fear for I'm your God. I'll give you strength. I'll help you. I'll hold you steady, keep a firm grip on you" (Isaiah 41:10). Looking back, I know this was true.

What I Have Learned

The only way out of the pain is through it. I had to keep moving through the process. Here are some important things, I've learned as I walked through the process of dealing with life after receiving the devastating news of my husband's terminal condition. I pray they will help you in your journey as well.

Don't give up on your life. Stay in touch with people and continue to handle matters in your own life as much as possible.

Do not focus solely on the issue of death. Try to stay balanced by also thinking and talking about the life you have had together. There may come times when your loved one tells you what a strong person you are, that's why I married you. Memories are powerful. Don't be afraid to throw in a little humor, playfulness, give a smile, wink, and perhaps even tell them why you married them. There may be other times when the stress is overwhelming and you need to find an outlet for the pain.

Express your emotions. It may or may not be wise to completely download on your loved one, but don't feel you have to hide every emotion from him or her. Find someone to confide in when you need to do a major download to release those emotions. In my case, there were times I had to find an object to throw, a pillow to punch, or a place I could escape to and just scream; anything to air out my brain and emotions.

Set aside some quiet time to pray and meditate every day. Go and sit on the Father's lap and allow Him to bring you what you need to carry on.

Prepare for sudden changes. I didn't realize it at the time, but situations can change rapidly in the case of a terminally-ill loved one. A change in the condition of the loved one can alter plans or call for drastic action. Be aware, there may be quality-of-life changes in the time to come.

Bringing the immediate family (our son and daughter) helped a lot. We found it to be calming and protective. I noticed how it brought peace to my husband to be able to say goodbye. Then on November 5, 2010, when my husband crossed over into a better place of rest for his spirit, we were all there.

CHAPTER SEVEN

Overcome and Reclaim Your Purpose

My Story

I recall one year I bought my husband a little Valentine figurine that said, "Loving You Is What I Do Best." I wanted this to be one of my greatest achievements. I desired to be my husband's soulmate and helpmate. God created the first marriage in the Garden of Eden because He said, "It is not good that man should be alone; I will make him a helper comparable to him" (Genesis 2:18). Eve was not meant to be a slave. She was meant to serve with her life's partner.

However, it's so easy to slide into a dull humdrum routine and maintain a status quo in a marriage. Love must continue to grow. This growth needs to be balanced in all three areas of our lives—spiritual, psychological, and physical. Spiritually, God wants us to grow up into Him together as husband and wife. Although we may be different in temperament, our basic beliefs and goals must be the same if we are going to grow together.

We should feel comfortable praying with each other, discussing spiritual things, and serving the Lord together. As we grow together in Christ, we will be able to help one another more and more. Then when life's storms come along, we can stand together as we weather the struggles of life knowing God is right there with us every step of the way.

Psychological growth means that a truly smart woman will never pit her intelligence or wit against the man she loves. She will build him up, causing him to become the man God has called him to be as head of their household. There are many areas where she can excel without "locking horns" with her husband. This is especially true when you are called to face challenges like a diagnosis of a terminal disease. Working together will make the journey easier for both spouses.

Physically, we need to continue to take good care of ourselves and honor both God and our spouse by looking and feeling healthy and strong. Though it may be hard to remember this in the midst of the demands of caring for a terminally-ill spouse, it is vital we take the time to care for our own health as well.

Enjoy your marriage. God has blessed you with your spouse. None of us are guaranteed how long we will have with one another. Live life to the fullest with each other and rejoice in every day you have together. You do not want to face life after the loss of your spouse regretting you were too busy to enjoy them while they were still with you. Make memories you can hold onto for the rest of your journey to fulfill your purpose in God.

Key Points and Scriptures

Not everyone responds in exactly the same way to hard times in his or her personal life. However, we don't have to be discouraged or depressed. What does 1 Peter 3:12 assure you?

You do not have to be paralyzed by the storms of life. What did Jesus say in Matthew 7:25 that will help you through the storm you are facing in your life?

What is the answer to the storms of life, the swirling winds, the torrential life, particularly when it involves the imminent death of a loved one?

Take a moment to review and meditate on the list of what I learned about dealing with the diagnosis that involves the imminent death of your loved one:

1. Don't give up on your life (every moment is precious).

2. Do not focus solely on the issue of death (follow their lead).

3. Set aside some quiet time to pray and meditate every day (at least try).

4. Prepare for sudden changes (no warning signs at every crossroad).

5. Pray about everything.

6. Enjoy your marriage (avoid any regrets).

Prayer: *Heavenly Father, I know in my heart these tears will one day give way again to joy, yet for now I know only pain. Help me find the courage to let these tears flow, to feel the loss and heartbreak as You walk me through this storm, so that I may come out whole and cleansed again. Thank You that on the outside of my sorrow I know life waits for me. I want to laugh again, be strong and confident so that I can serve You as I move ahead with my life.*

> *God bless you and keep you, God smile on you and gift you, God look you full in the face and make you prosper.*

(Numbers 6:24-26)

To go through, here are ten tips I found helpful to overcome my own grief journey:

1. Be honest with your feelings.

2. Find positive ways to express your feelings.

3. Talk to a trusted friend.

4. Read books on grief.

5. Know that it is okay to ask tough questions.

6. Seek out a local Hospice or Grief-Share program.

7. Do something special to honor your loved one's memory.

8. Each day, if you can, write a gratitude list.

9. Practice healthy lifestyle choices.

10. Give yourself permission to not rush through grief.

CHAPTER EIGHT

Conquering and Caring for the Bereaved

One should never grieve alone. Family and friends are there to uphold you in your time of grieving. Some will know how to support and minister to you because they truly understand what you are going through. They may offer counsel or just sit beside you or hold you when you need a hug. Others may not know how to minister to you directly, but will offer their assistance in other ways such as keeping track of the flowers and food offerings. Some may offer to contact family members, help with housing out-of-town family, or do airport runs. You need to allow them to do these things as it is their way to offer their condolences. Someone who is a good organizer can take a lot off your shoulders as you prepare to move on after the death of your loved one.

God Knows What You Need

Please remember, our God reminds us He will never leave us nor forsake us. He will send help through people who have walked the grief journey before you. God will also use the messages others may send us. He will send us teachers or ministers from our churches or music to minister and encourage us as we go through this grieving process. He knows what we need and when we need it.

Though the days ahead seem hopeless, overwhelming, and dark, we must be careful not to allow ourselves to shut ourselves up and crawl into a cocoon to isolate ourselves completely from others. We will need some alone time, but too much isolation can turn into dangerous depression. Our days may become long and dreary, leaving us with no desire to answer the phone, open the door, or pull back the drapes. These actions, coupled with solitary disparaging thoughts may take over our minds and hearts. We may even find ourselves in a battle with the Lord. If these things happen, we may need to seek professional help. The brokenness we are experiencing will go through multiple cycles including anger, sadness, and guilt. We need to know it is okay to vent to our Heavenly Father. Give yourself permission to cry as you openly and honestly share with Him all that you are experiencing.

God wants you to know He's your Father, and has everything you will need to walk through the valley of the shadow of death and come out in victory with Him by your side. He will mend your broken heart and show you how to move forward into a productive and full life.

"I'll convert their weeping into laughter, lavishing comfort, invading their grief with joy..."
declares the Lord.

(Jeremiah 31:13)

Ready or not, family and friends will move on. There will be no more calls, cards, or visits. They have moved on and believe you should be doing fine whether or not that is true. Friends and loved ones will hint that it's time to move on. Remember, though, everyone handles grief differently; there is no set timeframe; there is no set order to the grieving process, and there is no complete healing without God as your guide and comfort. Do not be afraid to seek counsel if you feel you are not able to move forward or are unable to function in a healthy lifestyle.

Even when you begin to believe you're doing better, one small reminder through a song, an object or you may just find yourself reflecting on a special event from your past—all and any of that—could awaken those intense feelings of grief again. It's natural, it will happen. You need to allow the process to take its course and not become impatient with yourself.

Returning to life as usual no longer exists. Expecting that to happen is just going to cause you to get frustrated with yourself. Even as your life at home begins to become your new normal, reporting back to work will start the process all over again. Having to repeat the cycle as you receive condolences from co-workers can cause what might feel like a setback to you. Going to the hairdresser, shopping at your local store, and any other places you have frequented in the past can cause anxiety as you anticipate the questions and expressions of concern from those who know about your loss.

Adjusting or learning how to manage things for the first time can be a tremendous shock and set one back no matter where you are in the grieving and healing process. Even when you find yourself seeking help from family and friends, it can be difficult to express your feelings about all the overwhelming events that have occurred in your life. Take things one day at a time and allow friends and neighbors to encourage and comfort you. Give yourself time, but seek comfort and help, as you need to, from those the Lord has sent. To care for the needs of all who mourn in Zion, give them bouquets of roses instead of ashes (Isaiah 61:3).

Family and Friends Dos and Don'ts

Whether or not the loss of a loved one happened through an accidental death, suicide, illness, or due to natural causes, you can respond in ways that will support their unique needs.
What NOT to do...

Don't feel like you have to constantly be talking. Just being there to listen can help.

Don't fill in conversation with outside news. Other topics can overshadow the mourner's grief.

Don't use this as an opportunity to convert your friend or family member to your spiritual beliefs. Don't use clichés to try to console.

Don't talk about your own losses or problems.

Don't try to take the place of the deceased.

Don't impose a time limit on your support.

Don't shy away from conversations or stories that involve the deceased.

What to do...

Acknowledge the death.

Refer to the deceased by name.

Be there to listen. Let the bereaved talk about their feelings. Don't worry about how you are going to respond, just try to be understanding.

Allow your loved one to talk about the deceased. Perhaps you've heard the story before, but be patient. Remembering can be helpful.

Let your friend know that you would like to spend time with them when they are ready, but don't impose on them if they would like to be alone.

Allow and encourage others to help. It's important for a grieving person to have a wide network of support.

Commit to contacting your friend on a regular basis–once a week or once a month.

Take your friend out to have fun so they can see that life still holds many pleasures.

Proactively clean, cook, or do other chores. Offering to help is generous and appreciated, but the bereaved are often hesitant to take up volunteers on their offers.

If your friend remains depressed for a long period of time, find a tactful way to suggest therapy. Many people reject this idea, but it can help.

Remember, it can take a long time for a grieving person to feel normal again, so don't expect one visit to cause a change of heart. The most important part of helping a grieving person is being there when they need you, so make yourself available.

The moment that you died
My heart was torn in two,
One side filled with heartache,
The other died with you.
I often lie awake at night,
When the world is fast asleep,
And take a walk down memory lane,
With tears upon my cheeks.
Remembering you is easy,
I do it every day,
But missing you is heartache,
That never goes away.
I hold you tightly within my heart,
And there you will remain
Until the joyous day arrives,
That we will meet again.

-Unknown

CONCLUSION

My Test Is My Testimony

*If your heart is broken, you'll find God right there; if
you're kicked in the gut, he'll help you catch your breath.*

(Psalm 34:18)

When we received the confirmation of my husband's terminal diagnosis, the knowledge of his pending death took command of my thoughts. I was brokenhearted. It literally felt like my heart was shattering into many pieces. On the night of my dear husband's death, I knelt beside him, trembling, and shaking, as I embraced him in my arms, but he didn't embrace me back.

With my mouth wide open, I screamed, "Lord, Lord, Oh Lord, how could this be?"

With my eyes gazing upwards toward the sky, all I could do was cry. Frozen in position, unable to move, I tightly gripped the one I knew. I felt as though I was suffocating and struggling to breathe. Inhaling and exhaling was nearly impossible. The weight on my chest felt like a ton. There was nothing more I could do.

I cried out, "Son, come please come."

He entered the room, looked over at his father, and cried out, "Dad!"

He draped his entire body over his father's and wept.

My daughter called out, "Is everything all right?"

I answered, "Dad is dead."

She ran up the stairs, speaking in a whispered tone, "Oh no."

She ran over to her father's side, but I could see that she was unable to connect, directly, to a part of his body. She leaned over her brother and began to cry.

> *No test or temptation that comes your way is beyond*
> *the course of what others have had to face. All you need*
> *to remember is that God will never let you down; he'll*
> *never let you be pushed past your limit; he'll always be*
> *there to help you come through it.*

(1 Corinthians 10:13)

God promised He will not let us be tested beyond what our strength can handle. In my case, my test has become my testimony, not just for me but for others. My test taught me death is a part of life. It's already established, mandated, and set up by God. The Message Bible says in Hebrews 9:27, "Everyone has to die once, then face the consequences. Christ's death was also a one-time event, but it was a sacrifice that took care of sins forever."

While we are still here on the Earth, God will give us what we need to accomplish what He has now called us to do. He will equip a widow like me to speak to another widow to let her know her pain is my pain, her brokenness is my brokenness, and my beauty for ashes will be her beauty for ashes. I hope through sharing my loss, my brokenness, and my pain, someone will see their beauty for ashes to let the healing process take place in their life. I pray by sharing my test and my testimony, another will come to Christ or move closer to Christ so they can go through their own grief, pain, and pressure, to reclaim God's purpose for their life.

Broken Chain

We little knew that morning that God was going to call your name.

In life we loved you dearly, in death we do the same.

It broke our hearts to lose you, yet you did not go alone;

For part of us went with you, the day God called you home.

You left us peaceful memories, your love is still our guide;

And though we cannot see you, you are always at our side.

Our family chain is broken, and nothing seems the same;

But as God calls us one by one, the chain will link again.

-Unknown

Prayer: *Lord, lead me to the life You have planned for me. Unravel the strands of confusion and weave together a course that is of Your design. This new vision of my life involves asking You for directions, for I treasure Your perfect will. Thank You for the miracles of life and a sky so blue that reflects peace. Thank You for dear family and friends so strong, they mirror Your faithfulness. Thank You for happiness so deep it encompasses Your joy. Because You are at the core of all these miracles of life, I know that Your love for me is more vibrant. Lord, I praise Your presence in every remarkable thing. Your radiance illuminates the miraculous in each moment and You continue to remind me of the beautiful pattern my steps create when I seek You. I sing praises to You all the day long. My lips glorify You constantly; You deserve it; You are worthy; and there is nothing better than Your love. Made in Your image, fearlessly and wondrously, I am Your daughter, the apple of Your eye.*

REFERENCES FOR STRENGTH

Here is a list of the Bible verses I used to inspire and comfort me during my times of need as I walked through the grief, pain, and pressure. During your quiet moments, read, meditate, and record in your journal what the Lord is sharing with you.

Anger

1 Timothy 2:8 – Since prayer is at the bottom of all this, what I want mostly is for men to pray—not shaking angry fists at enemies but raising holy hands to God.

Ephesian 4:26–Go ahead and be angry. You do well to be angry—but don't use your anger as fuel for revenge.

Matthew 5:21-22 – You're familiar with the command to the ancients, 'Do not murder.' I'm telling you that anyone who is so much as angry with a brother or sister is guilty of murder. Carelessly call a brother 'idiot!' and you just might find yourself hauled into court. Thoughtlessly yell 'stupid!' at a sister and you are on the brink of hellfire. The simple moral fact is that words kill.

Ecclesiastes 7:9 – Don't be quick to fly off the handle. Anger boomerangs. You can spot a fool by the lumps on his head.

Proverbs 27:4 – We're blasted by anger and swamped by rage, but who can survive jealousy?

Proverbs 22:24-25 –Don't hang out with angry people; don't' keep company with hotheads. Bad temper is contagious—don't get infected.

Proverbs 15:1 – A gentle response defuses anger, but a sharp tongue kindles a temper-fire.

Proverbs 14:17 – The hotheaded do things they'll later regret: the cold-hearted get the cold shoulder.

Psalm 37:8 – Bridle your anger, trash your wrath, cool your pipes—it only makes things worse.

Psalm 4:4 – Complain if you must, but don't lash out. Keep your mouth shut, and let your heart do the talking.

Death

Revelation 2:11 -Are your ears awake? Listen. Listen to the Wind Words, the Spirit blowing through the churches. Christ-conquerors are safe from Devil-death.

Philippians 1:22-26 – As long as I'm alive in this body, there is good work for me to do. If I had to choose right now, I hardly know which I'd choose. Hard choice! The desire to break camp here and be with Christ is powerful. Some days I can think of nothing better. But most days, because of what you are going throught, I am sure that it's better for me to stick it out here. So I plan to be around awhile, companion to you as your growth and joy in this life of trusting God continues. You can start looking forward to a great reunion when I come visit you again. We'll be praising Christ, enjoying each other.

2 Corinthians 5:8 – Do you suppose few a ruts in the road or rocks in the path are going to stop us? When the time comes, we'll be plenty ready to exchange exile for homecoming.

1 Corinthians 15:51-52 – But let me tell you something wonderful, a mystery I'll probably never fully understand. We're not all going to die— but we are all going to be changed. You hear a blast to end all blasts from a trumpet, and in the time that you look up and blink your eyes— it's over.

Romans 6:23 – A whole, healed, put-together life right now, with more and more of life on the way! Work hard for sin your whole life and your pension is death. But God's gift is real life, eternal life, delivered by Jesus, our Master.

John 3:16 –This is how much God loved the world: He gave his Son, his one and only son. And this is why: so that no one need be destroyed; by believing in him anyone can have a whole and lasting life.

Palm 33:18-19 – Watch this: God's eye is on those who respect him, the ones who are looking for his love. He's already to come to their rescue in bad times; in lean times he keeps body and soul together.

Depression

Ecclesiastes 7:3-5 – Crying is better than laughing. It blotches the face but it scours the heart. Sages invest themselves in hurt and grieving. Fools waste their lives in fun and games. You'll get more from the rebuke of a sage. Than from the song and dance of fools.

Proverbs 14:13 – Sure, those people appear to be having a good time, but all that laughter will end in heartbreak.

Psalm 94:18-19 – If God hadn't been there for me, I never would have made it. The minute I said, "I'm slipping, I'm falling," your love, God, took hold and held me fast. When I was upset and beside myself, you calmed me down and cheered me up.

Psalm 56:8-11 – You've kept track of my every toss and turn through the sleepless nights, each tear entered in your ledger, each ache written in your book. If my enemies run away, turn tail when I yell at them, Then I'll know that God is on my side. I'm proud to praise God, proud to praise God. Fearless now, I trust in God; what can mere mortals do to me?

Discouragement

Hebrews 10:25 – Let's see how inventive we can be in encouraging love and helping out, not avoiding worshiping together as some do but spurring each other on, especially as we see the big Day approaching.

Hebrews 3:12-14 – So watch your step, friends. Make sure there's no evil unbelief lying around that will trip you up and throw you off course, diverting you from the living God. For as long as it's still God's Today, keep each other on your toes so sin doesn't slow down your reflexes. If we can only keep our grip on the sure thing we started out with, we're in this with Christ for the long haul. These words keep ringing in our ears: Today, please listen; don't turn a deaf ear as in the bitter uprising.

Colossians 2:1 – I want you to realize that I continue to work as hard as I know how for you, and also for the Christians over at Laodicea. Not many of you have met me face-to-face, but that doesn't make any difference. Know that I'm on your side, right alongside you. You're not in this alone.

Isaiah 1:17 – Say no to wrong. Learn to do good. Work for justice. Help the down-and-out. Stand up for the homeless. Go to bat for the defenseless.

Esther 4:13-16 – Don't think that just because you live in the king's house you're the one Jew who will get out of this alive. If you persist in staying silent at a time like this, help and deliverance will arrive for the Jews from someplace else; but you and your family will be wiped out. Who knows? Maybe you were made queen for just such a time as this.

Fear

Psalm 23:4 – Even when the way goes through Death Valley, I'm not afraid when you walk at my side. Your trusty shepherd's crook makes me feel secure.

Luke 12:4-5 – "I'm speaking to you as dear friends. Don't be bluffed into silence or insincerity by the threats of religious bullies. True, they can kill you, but then what can they do? There's nothing they can do to your soul, your core being. Save your fear for God, who holds your entire life—body and soul—in his hands.

Philippians 2:12-13 – What I'm getting at, friends, is that you should simple keep on doing what you've done from the beginning. When I was living among you, you lived in responsive obedience. Now that I'm separated from you, keep it up. Better yet, redouble your efforts. Be energetic in your life of salvation, reverent and sensitive before God. That energy is God's energy, and energy deep within you, God himself willing and working at what will give him the most pleasure.

2 Timothy 1:5-7 – That precious memory triggers another: your grandmother Lois to your mother Eunice, and now to you! And the special gift of ministry you received when I laid hands on you and prayed— keep that ablaze! God doesn't want us to be shy with his gifts, but bold and loving and sensible.

Suffering

Book of Job

1 Peter 2:19-21 – There's no particular virtue in accepting punishment that you will deserve. But if you're treated badly for good behavior and continue in spite of it to be a good servant, that is what counts with God. This is the kind of life you've been invited into, the kind of life Christ lived. He suffered everything that came his way so you would know that it can be done, and also know how to do it, step-by-step.

2 Corinthians 1:3-5 – All praise to the God and Father of our Master, Jesus the Messiah! Father of all mercy! God of all healing counsel! He comes alongside us when we go through hard times, and before you know it, he brings us alongside someone else who is going through hard times so that we can be there for that person just as God was there for us. We have plenty of hard times that come from following the Messiah, but no more so than the good times of his healing comfort—we get a full measure of that, too.

Romans 5:3-5 – There's more to come: We continue to shout our praise even when we're hemmed in what troubles, because we know how troubles can develop passionate patience in us, and how that patience in turn forges the tempered steel of virtue, keeping us alert for whatever God will do next. In alert expectancy such as this, we're never left feeling shortchanged. Quite the contrary—we can't round up enough containers to hold everything God generously pours into our lives through the Holy Spirit.

Worry

Philippians 4:6-7 – Don't fret or worry. Instead of worrying, pray. Let petitions and praises shape your worries into prayers, letting God know your concerns. Before you know it, a sense of God's wholeness, everything coming together for good, will come and settle you down. It's wonderful what happens when Christ displaces worry at the center of your life.

Matthew 10:21-23 – When people realize it is the living God you are presenting and not some idol that makes them feel good, they are going to turn on you, even people in your own family. There is a great irony here: proclaiming so much love, experiencing so much hate! But don't quit. Don't cave in. It is all well worth it in the end. It is not success you are after in such time but survival. Be survivors! Before you've run out of options, the Son of Man will have arrived.

Psalm 139:23-24 – Investigate my life, O God, find out everything about me; Cross-examine and test me, get a clear picture of what I'm about; See for yourself whether I've done anything wrong—then guide me on the road to eternal life.

About the Author

Rita A. Wallace-Posey is a widow, Federal government retiree, Self-employed Entrepreneur and an author. Ms. Wallace-Posey is a member of The National Association for Professional Women (NAPW), the Life Journeys Writers Guild, Inc., Southern Maryland Minority Chamber of Commerce (SMMCOC), National Association for the Advancement of Colored People (NAACP), former board member of The Charles County Commission for Women, and an active volunteer in her community. She is also a committed, loving, and devoted mother and grandmother living in Maryland. She cherishes and enjoys every moment with her family and friends. Ms. Wallace-Posey is grateful for a rebirth of life and more...